EARLY ITALIAN KEYBOARD MUSIC

49 Works by Frescobaldi, Scarlatti, Martini and Others

Edited by
M. Esposito

DOVER PUBLICATIONS, INC.
Mineola, New York

Bibliographical Note

This Dover edition, first published in 2005, is a republication of *Early Italian Piano Music,* originally published by the Oliver Ditson Company, Boston, 1906. In the interest of space, a brief preliminary section introducing the clavichord and harpsichord has been omitted.

International Standard Book Number: 0-486-44188-1

Manufactured in the United States of America
Dover Publications, Inc., 31 East 2nd Street, Mineola, N.Y. 11501

CONTENTS

CONTENTS

ITALIAN COMPOSERS FOR THE
HARPSICHORD

IN the sixteenth century Italy was first in all the arts, in music, in sculpture, in painting and in literature. Palestrina was called upon to reform church music, and he composed masses of a beauty that has never been equalled; Luca Marenzio composed his madrigals, and Monteverde invented the opera. The example of these geniuses was followed by a host of lesser composers; schools for music were founded, and French, Belgian and Spanish musicians, who one hundred years before had gone to Italy to teach, now came to learn and to admire. Though a great deal of the music written in Italy in the sixteenth century was vocal,—all Palestrina's masses, in fact all religious music was unaccompanied,—instrumental composition was not neglected, and at the beginning of the seventeenth century Frescobaldi produced his works for *Organo e Cembalo*, and later on Corelli and Viotti wrote for the violin.

That the musical inspiration which arose in Italy in the sixteenth century should have been continued far into the eighteenth shows how strong the instinct must have been, and how excellent the musical tradition; and the learning of these masters of old time, and their knowledge of music, will, I think, astonish the reader of this volume. I have endeavored to bring together, for the student and the amateur, examples of the music that was written at this time for the harpsichord. They have been chosen from the earliest Italian composers down to Clementi, whom I have included, although he has written chiefly for the modern pianoforte.

True it is that most of these pieces have been published in various editions, but Alessandro Scarlatti's toccatas are given now for the first time by the kind permission of the authorities of the Conservatorio di Musica Giuseppe Verdi, of Milan, where the original manuscripts are kept.

The pieces of this volume follow the originals strictly, and whenever I have thought it necessary to make a slight alteration the altered passage is given together with the original. I have supplied the marks for expression and speed, for, as every one knows, those old composers only put the mere notes on the paper. I claim no more for my marks of expression than that they were suggested to me by the music, and every one is free to alter them according to his individual feeling.

BIOGRAPHICAL SKETCHES

ERCOLE PASQUINI was born in Ferrara about 1580. He studied with one of the Milleville, who were established at the Court of the Duke of Ferrara. Pasquini was organist at San Pietro in Rome; he left Rome in 1614, but his reasons for leaving and what became of him are unknown. He was a celebrated organist; but his compositions are rare, and few are acquainted with them.

Frescobaldi succeeded him at San Pietro.

GIROLAMO FRESCOBALDI was born in Ferrara in 1583, and was buried in Rome, March 2, 1644. He was a pupil of Luzzasco Luzzaschi, and when, accompanied by his master, he went to Rome, to fill the place left vacant by Ercole Pasquini, a crowd of thirty thousand people assembled to hear him play the organ in the Cathedral. He left works that place him above all composers of his time for the organ and cembalo or harpsichord. His toccatas, canzonas, fugues, &c., are full of beautiful melodies and daring harmonies, and show an extraordinary feeling of tonality. Besides the technical difficulties of his compositions Frescobaldi wrote on a stave of *six* lines for the right hand and *eight* lines for the left. (See illustration below.)

In the preface to his *Toccate d' intavolatura di cembalo ed organo* Frescobaldi, after having protested that he prefers the merits of other composers to his own, proceeds to give some advice on the playing of his compositions: that the time must not be kept with strict beats throughout, but be subjected to the emotion, sentiment and brilliancy of the different passages; that the opening of the toccata be played slow, and the chords and discords *arpeggiando;* that the cadenzas, although written rapidly, must be played broadly and *rallentando* towards the end; that melodic passages be played slowly, and brilliant ones quickly; and, finally, that he leaves to the good taste and judgment of the player full liberty in selecting the *tempo,* "in which consists the spirit and perfection of this manner and style of playing."

MICHELANGELO ROSSI was born in Rome; the date of his birth is unknown, but it is certain that he lived there from 1620 to 1660. He was a pupil of Frescobaldi, and

had a great reputation as a violinist, organist and composer. In 1625 an opera written by him, *Erminia sul Giordano,* was performed in Rome, and successfully. His book called *Intavolatura d'organo e cembalo,* published in Rome, 1657, contains many interesting pieces. We find in the *Toccata in D minor* (see page 21) many daring modulations, and its close is an extraordinary example of the early use of chromatics. The *Andantino* (see page 18) might have been written by a Mozart.

BERNARDO PASQUINI was born in Massa de Valnevola, Tuscany, the 8th of December, 1637. He studied with Loreto Vittori and Antonio Cesti. When quite a young man he was appointed organist in Santa Maria Maggiore in Rome, and later organist of the Senate and Roman People. He was the greatest organist of Italy in the latter part of the seventeenth century, and his best pupils were F. Gasperini and Francesco Durante. He died in Rome on the 22d of November, 1710.

ALESSANDRO SCARLATTI, one of the greatest of Italian composers, was born in Trapani, Sicily, in 1649. He studied counterpoint under Carissimi in Rome, and later became

maestro di cappella of Queen Christine of Sweden, then living in Rome. In 1688, after the Queen's death, he accepted a similar appointment at the Chapel Royal of Naples. In 1703 he went back to Rome as *maestro di cappella* of Santa Maria Maggiore, where he stayed until March, 1709, and then returned to Naples. He died there October 24, 1725.

In the various *conservatori di musica* of Naples (Sant' Onofrio, Poveri di Gesù Cristo, Loreto) he taught many who became celebrated and contributed to the glory of the Neapolitan school; for instance, Logroscino, Durante, and his own son Domenico.

Alessandro Scarlatti was a voluminous writer: one hundred and fifteen operas, two hundred masses, several oratorios, a large number of cantatas, church music, chamber music, &c. Many of his compositions for the harpsichord are still unpublished; a *Fugue in F minor* and an *Allegro in G major* have been printed in collections of music by old composers. Fétis, however, speaks of two books of toccatas and a suite of pieces. Through the kindness of the authorities of the Milan Conservatorio di Musica Giuseppe Verdi, I was permitted to copy ten toccatas for the harpsichord, with a view to publication; and some of these pieces are now printed for the first time. I felt I must harmonize the *Aria* from *Toccata Seconda* and the *Minuetto* from *Toccata Quarta*, for in the originals only the melody and the bass are given; no doubt the composer left the performer free to harmonize it, the ♯ on the two B's in the bass being, I hope, my valid excuse. All the other toccatas are left as in the originals. I wish to call the attention of musicians to *Toccata Settima*.

The form of Scarlatti's toccatas is quite different from those of Frescobaldi and Rossi, which may be almost said to be formless and read like improvisations. Every one of Scarlatti's toccatas is different; but though he changes the form, there is always form.

No. 1 is in one movement, not unlike his son's pieces.

No. 2 is in four movements: *Adagio, Allegro, Grave (aria), Vivace.*

No. 3 is in two movements· *Allegro, Giga.*

No. 4 is in three movements: *Allegro, Adagio, Minuetto.*

No. 5 is in three movements: *Allegro, Adagio, Alla Francese.*

No. 6 is in one movement.

No. 7 is a theme with variations.

No. 8 is in two movements: *Allegro, Giga.*

No. 9 is in one movement, like a fantasia.

No. 10 is in one movement.

From the above it will be seen that Scarlatti gave a wider meaning to the name "toccata." In some of these pieces he wrote what we would call a small sonata, in two, three or four movements.

The best of these pieces to my mind is No. 7, *Tema con variazioni.* He seems to have been the inventor of this form, for we do not find it in the works of any earlier composer, nor in any later until we come to Beethoven. The theme is in itself a strong one; and the treatment, the technique, the handling of each variation, are extraordinary. With later composers these would be mere scales, arpeggios or florid passages; but with Scarlatti there is a sequence of rhythm and mood, and we have a sense that the composer is working up to a complete whole. The closes of the second, third, fourth, sixth and eighth variations are full of passion, such as we find in no one else before Beethoven. In looking at this toccata and at No. 9 one can hardly realize that such music was written merely for the cembalo at a time when Bach and Handel were still boys, and one hundred years before Beethoven.

CARLO FRANCESCO POLLAROLO, born in Brescia about the middle of the seventeenth century, studied with Legrenzi, and passed all his life in Venice, where he died in 1722. He composed seventy operas, various oratorios, cantatas and organ pieces. The fugue given in this volume is a good specimen of his vigorous writing.

DOMENICO SCARLATTI, son of the great Alessandro Scarlatti, was born in Naples, in 1683. His father was his first teacher; and later he went to Rome and finished his studies under Gasparini. He became Italy's greatest harpsichord player, and one of the best in Europe. He wrote several operas, and they were all performed in Italy. When he visited London, in 1720, his opera *Narciso* was given at the Italian Opera. Scarlatti also composed church music, but it is his pieces for the harpsichord which place him in the first rank of composers for that instrument. Many and varied ideas, charming melodies and abundance of technical devices make these pieces a source of continual delight to musicians and amateurs. Any one of them may be placed on a modern pianoforte-recital programme with a certainty of pleasing the audience. Scarlatti wrote a great number of pieces for the harpsichord; about five hundred have been attributed to him. Some have been printed, but many remain still in manuscript.

Domenico Scarlatti died at Naples in 1757.

FRANCESCO DURANTE was born in Frattamaggiore in the kingdom of Naples, March 15, 1684. He was admitted into the Conservatorio dei Poveri di Gesù Cristo and became a pupil of Gaetano Greco, and soon acquired great ability as player on the harpsichord and organ. Later on he was sent to the Conservatorio di S. Onofrio, and finished his studies with Alessandro Scarlatti. He composed chiefly church music, and his compositions were admired all over Europe. To him, more than to any other Neapolitan teacher, is due the foundation of the famous Neapolitan school of the eighteenth century, and his pupils included Traetta, Vinci, Jomelli, Piccini, Sacchini, Guglielmi and Paisiello.

He became professor at the Conservatorio di Loreto, in Naples, in 1742, and died August 13, 1755.

BENEDETTO MARCELLO, the celebrated composer of the *Psalms*, was born in Venice, July 24, 1686. He was of noble birth, and received a solid and manifold education; but poetry and music attracted him, and he studied counterpoint with Gasperini, for whom he had great respect.

Like all Venetian nobles, Marcello, in his young days, studied law and held several posts as magistrate. For fourteen years he was member of the Council of the Forty, and was sent as "Provvisore" to Pola in 1730. There his health broke down, and in 1738 he went to Brescia (as treasurer), hoping the change would benefit him. Unfortunately he did not recover his health, and he died there on the 24th of July, 1739.

Besides his fifty celebrated *Psalms* he composed some dramatic works, masses, oratorios, cantatas and instrumental music. The toccata published in this volume is remarkable for its peculiar wrist motion and clearness of form.

NICCOLÒ PORPORA was born in Naples, August 19, 1686. He studied at the Conservatorio di Santa Maria di Loreto under Gaetano Greco and others; and probably received advice from Alessandro Scarlatti. Like all Italian composers he wrote numerous operas, oratorios, masses, &c.; but his best compositions are his cantatas for solo voice with harpsichord accompaniments, twelve of which were published in London in 1735. He was a great teacher, and the most famous singers of the eighteenth century were his pupils, viz., Farinelli, Caffarelli, Porporino, Salimbeni and Molteni. In Vienna he gave a few lessons to young Haydn; in Dresden he met with ingratitude from his former pupil Hasse. In London he competed with Handel and founded a rival opera house; but his adventure was not successful, and he returned to Naples, old and in broken health, and died there, in poverty, in February, 1766. The fugue in this volume gives a good idea of his instrumental style.

DOMENICO ZIPOLI, born about 1686, was organist at the church of the Jesuits in Rome in the beginning of the eighteenth century. More than this is not known of his life, nor is the date of his death obtainable. He published in Rome, in 1716, *Sonate d' intavolatura d' organo e cembalo*. The two volumes in which his music is published contain many varied pieces, such as *toccate, versi, canzone, offertorî, pastorali, preludî, allemande, correnti, sarabande, gighe, gavotte* and *partite*. His style is flowing, melodic, elegant and harmonious.

GIAMBATTISTA MARTINI was born in Bologna, April 25, 1706. He was taught the violin at an early age by his father, who very soon found that there was nothing further he could teach the boy. Martini was sent to Padre Predieri, with whom he studied singing and harpsichord playing; Antonio Ricederi taught him counterpoint. He was confided to the Fathers of St. Filippo Neri for his moral and religious training, and they accomplished their task so well that when he was eighteen Martini became a monk.

He studied philosophy seriously, and acquired such a deep knowledge of theoretical and practical music that, although he was only nineteen, he was selected as *maestro di cappella* at the church of San Francesco. When not composing music he spent his time studying mathematics, and reading ancient and modern treatises on music. He gathered together a remarkable library of music-books and manuscripts. Martini collected for fifty years, and spent large sums on his collection. His former pupils, and foreign princes, his admirers, knowing his acquisitive passion, presented him with old and rare books and manuscripts, and vied with each other in increasing his collection.

Martini opened a School of Music in Bologna which soon became celebrated all over Europe, and the great musicians of his time were sensible of the advantages of his advice. He died October 3, 1784.

The greater part of Martini's compositions is still in manuscript at the Liceo Musicale, in Bologna; very little has ever been printed. He wrote masses, motets, oratorios and other kinds of religious and secular music. He also wrote eighteen sonatas for organ and harpsichord.

BALDASSARE GALUPPI was born October 18, 1706, in the island of Burano, near Venice. His father, who united the disparate offices of barber and violinist, was his first master. When he was sixteen he went to Venice and picked up a living by playing the organ in different churches. Galuppi was a daring boy, for though quite ignorant of the principles of music, he composed a comic opera, and was clever enough to get it performed; but he could not get it applauded,—it was hissed,—and in despair he resolved to return to the original shop, to the shears and the razor. But Benedetto Marcello, who recognized his musical talent, took the boy under his protection, and put him to learn counterpoint with Lotti. He also studied the harpsichord, and became a very good player. During his long life he composed many operas, all of which were performed in Italy, many with success, especially the comic ones. Catherine II sent for him, and he went to Russia, where his first opera, given in St. Petersburg, was well received. He returned to Italy, and died at Venice, in January, 1785.

PIETRO DOMENICO PARADIES was born in Naples about 1710, and studied with Porpora. He composed several operas, one of which was performed in London when he settled there as professor of the harpsichord in 1747. His twelve sonatas were published in London, in 1754, by John Johnson. Many years after he returned to Italy, and died in Venice about 1795.

FERDINANDO TURINI was born at Salo, near Brescia, in 1749. His uncle, F. Bertoni, taught him harmony and organ playing. At the age of twenty-three he lost his sight, was obliged to give up writing operas, and accepted a position as organist at the Church of Santa Giustina in Padova. In 1800, on account of the war, he went to Brescia, where he supported himself by teaching till his death, about 1812.

GIOVANNI BATTISTA GRAZIOLI was born in Venice about 1755, and studied with F. Bertoni, whom he succeeded as organist at. the Church of San Marco in 1782. He died in 1820. Several sonatas by Grazioli have been published in Germany.

MUZIO CLEMENTI was born in Rome in 1752, and died in England, March 10, 1832. With his *Gradus ad Parnassum* he laid the foundation of modern pianoforte playing. All his compositions, which include one hundred and five sonatas, belong to the period of pianoforte music and are outside the scope of this volume. Nevertheless I have decided to include his celebrated *Toccata* for comparison with those of the older composers. It would be useless to give any of his sonatas, as all students of the pianoforte are acquainted with them.

October 30, 1905.

EARLY ITALIAN
KEYBOARD MUSIC

CANZONA FRANCESE

Edited by M. Esposito

ERCOLE PASQUINI
(born about 1580)

2

Meno mosso (♩ = 72)

dolce

(a)

cresc.

p

cresc.

(a) In the original there is ═══ instead of the rest

TOCCATA, in G Minor

GIROLAMO FRESCOBALDI
(1588-1644)

Edited by M. Esposito

6

Allegro moderato (♩. = 144)

CORRENTE, in A Minor

Edited by M. Esposito

GIROLAMO FRESCOBALDI
(1583-1644)

GAGLIARDA, in G Minor

Edited by M. Esposito

GIROLAMO FRESCOBALDI
(1583-1644)

PIANO

PASSACAGLIA, in B♭ Major

Edited by M. Esposito

GIROLAMO FRESCOBALDI
(1583-1644)

PIANO

ARIA
(called "LA FRESCOBALDA")

Edited by M. Esposito

GIROLAMO FRESCOBALDI
(1583-1644)

VARIATION II (Gagliarda)

Energico (♩ = 132)

Part III

cresc.

stentato

14

VARIATION III
Andante con moto (♩ = 69)

Part IV

VARIATION IV (Corrente)
Graziosamente (♩ = 132)

Part V

FUGUE, in G Minor

Edited by M. Esposito

GIROLAMO FRESCOBALDI
(1583 - 1644)

Allegro moderato ($\bullet$ = 80)

PIANO

p espressivo

17

ANDANTINO, in G Major

Edited by M. Esposito

MICHELANGELO ROSSI
(died 1660)

TOCCATA, in D Minor

Edited by M. Esposito

MICHELANGELO ROSSI
(died 1660)

Moderato con espressione e molto legato (♩ = 69)

SONATA
(FUGUE)

Edited by M. Esposito

BERNARDO PASQUINI
(1637-1710)

*)ARIA
from "TOCCATA SECONDA"

Edited by M. Esposito

ALESSANDRO SCARLATTI
(1649 - 1725)

*) Harmonized by M. Esposito

★)MINUETTO
from "TOCCATA QUARTA"

Edited by M. Esposito

ALESSANDRO SCARLATTI
(1649 -1725)

★) Harmonized by M. Esposito

TEMA CON VARIAZIONI
(TOCCATA SETTIMA)

Edited by M. Esposito

ALESSANDRO SCARLATTI
(1649 - 1725)

VARIATION II

33

34

VARIATION V

leggieremente

VARIATION VIII

VARIATION IX
Vivamente ($\quad$ =100)

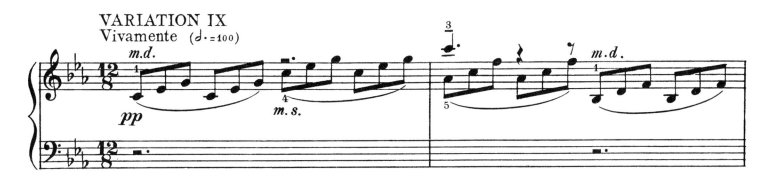

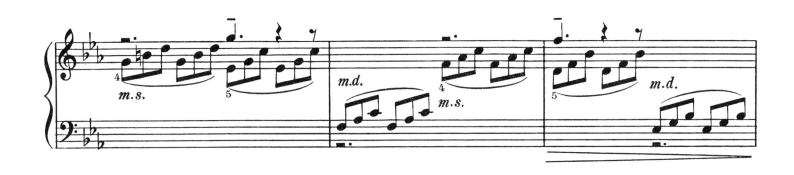

38

TOCCATA OTTAVA

Edited by M. Esposito

ALESSANDRO SCARLATTI
(1649 – 1725)

Allegro con brio ($\quad$ = 138)

PIANO

40

TOCCATA NONA

Edited by M. Esposito

ALESSANDRO SCARLATTI
(1649–1725)

PIANO

48

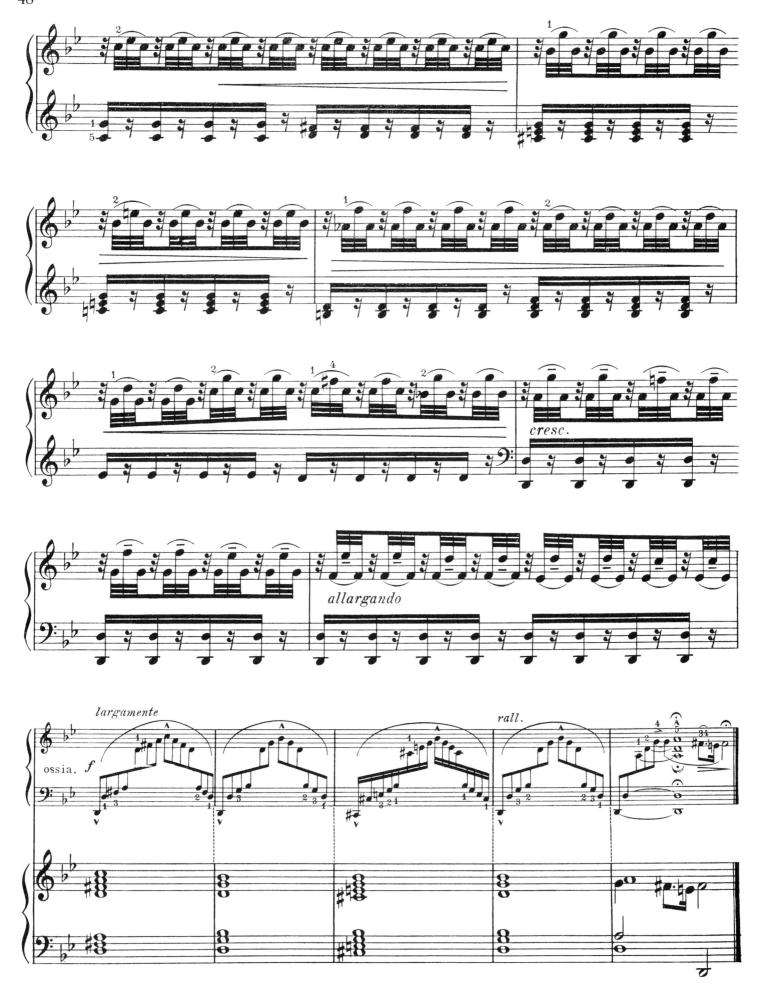

★)FUGUE, in F Minor

Edited by M. Esposito

ALESSANDRO SCARLATTI
(1649-1725)

★)Von Bülow wrongly ascribes this Fugue to Domenico Scarlatti

SONATA, in D Minor
(FUGUE)

Edited by M. Esposito

CARLO FRANCESCO POLLAROLI
(about 1650 - 1722)

Allegro con spirito ($\quad$ = 112)

PIANO

SONATA I, in D Major

Edited by M. Esposito

DOMENICO SCARLATTI
(1683–1757)

SONATA II
(TEMPO di BALLO)

Edited by M. Esposito

DOMENICO SCARLATTI
(1683–1757)

SONATA III, in G Minor

Edited by M. Esposito

DOMENICO SCARLATTI
(1683~1757)

SONATA IV, in G Minor

Edited by M. Esposito

DOMENICO SCARLATTI
(1683 - 1757)

un poco rit.   a tempo

SONATA V, in G Minor

Edited by M. Esposito

DOMENICO SCARLATTI
(1683 - 1757)

Allegro moderato (♩ = 92)

PIANO

SONATA VI, in G Major

Edited by M. Esposito

DOMENICO SCARLATTI
(1683 - 1757)

Allegro con brio (♩. = 132)

PIANO

f non legato e marcato

SONATA VII, in F Minor

Edited by M. Esposito

DOMENICO SCARLATTI
(1683 – 1757)

SONATA VIII, in F Major

Edited by M. Esposito

DOMENICO SCARLATTI
(1683–1757)

Allegretto pastorale ($\text{♩.}=69$)

PIANO

SONATA IX, in F Minor

Edited by M. Esposito

DOMENICO SCARLATTI
(1683-1757)

82

SONATA X, in F Major

Edited by M. Esposito

DOMENICO SCARLATTI

(1683 - 1757)

SONATA XI, in G Major

Edited by M. Esposito

DOMENICO SCARLATTI
(1683 – 1757)

SONATA XII, in G Minor

Edited by M. Esposito

DOMENICO SCARLATTI
(1683 - 1757)

SONATA XIII, in G Major

Edited by M. Esposito

DOMENICO SCARLATTI

(1683 - 1757)

Presto (♩. = 100)

PIANO

94

(a) In some editions the measures from (a) to (b) are omitted.

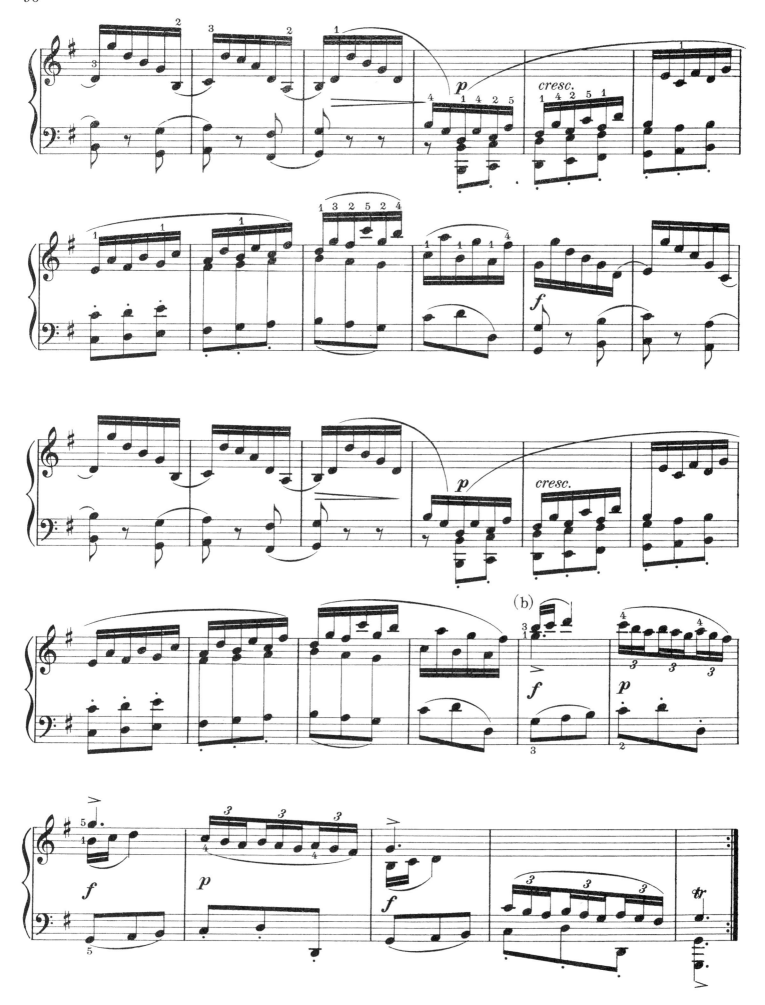

SONATA XIV, in C Major

Edited by M. Esposito

DOMENICO SCARLATTI
(1683-1757)

SONATA XV, in A Major

Edited by M. Esposito

DOMENICO SCARLATTI
(1683 - 1757)

102

SONATA XVI, in C Major

Edited by M. Esposito

DOMENICO SCARLATTI
(1683-1757)

SONATA XVII, in A Major

Edited by M. Esposito

DOMENICO SCARLATTI
(1683–1757)

PIANO

SONATA XVIII, in A Major

Edited by M. Esposito

DOMENICO SCARLATTI
(1683-1757)

PIANO

SONATA XIX, in D Minor

Edited by M. Esposito

DOMENICO SCARLATTI
(1683-1757)

THE CAT'S FUGUE

(FUGA DEL GATTO)

Edited by M. Esposito

DOMENICO SCARLATTI
(1683-1757)

One day the favorite cat of Scarlatti walked over the keyboard producing by chance the following notes: which the master used as the theme for a Fugue.

120

FUGUE, in F Minor
(STUDIO)

Edited by M. Esposito

FRANCESCO DURANTE.
(1684-1755)

TOCCATA, in C Minor

Edited by M. Esposito

BENEDETTO MARCELLO
(1686 - 1739)

FUGUE, in G Minor

Edited by M. Esposito

NICCOLO PORPORA
(1686-1766)

SUITE, in B Minor

PRELUDIO

Edited by M. Esposito

DOMENICO ZIPOLI
(born about 1686)

Lento con espressione (♩ = 72)

PIANO

CORRENTE

ARIA

140

GAVOTTA

ARIA
from the SONATA in C Minor

Edited by M. Esposito

PADRE GIAMBATTISTA MARTINI
(1706–1784)

GAVOTTA, in F Major

Edited by M Esposito

PADRE GIAMBATTISTA MARTINI
(1706-1784)

PRELUDIO and FUGUE, in E Minor

PRELUDIO

Edited by M. Esposito

PADRE GIAMBATTISTA MARTINI
(1706–1784)

150

FUGUE

SONATA, in D Major

Edited by M. Esposito

BALDASSARE GALUPPI
(1706–1785)

158

GIGUE
Presto con fuoco (♩. = 184)

SONATA, in A Major

Edited by M. Esposito

PIETRO DOMENICO PARADIES
(1710-1795)

PRESTO, in G Minor

Edited by M. Esposito

FERDINANDO TURINI
(1749–1812)

PIANO

(8i_a bassa)

MINUETTO
from the SONATA in G Major

Edited by M. Esposito

GIOVANNI BATTISTA GRAZIOLI
(1755-1820)

TOCCATA, in B♭ Major

Edited by M. Esposito

MUZIO CLEMENTI
(1752–1832)

PIANO

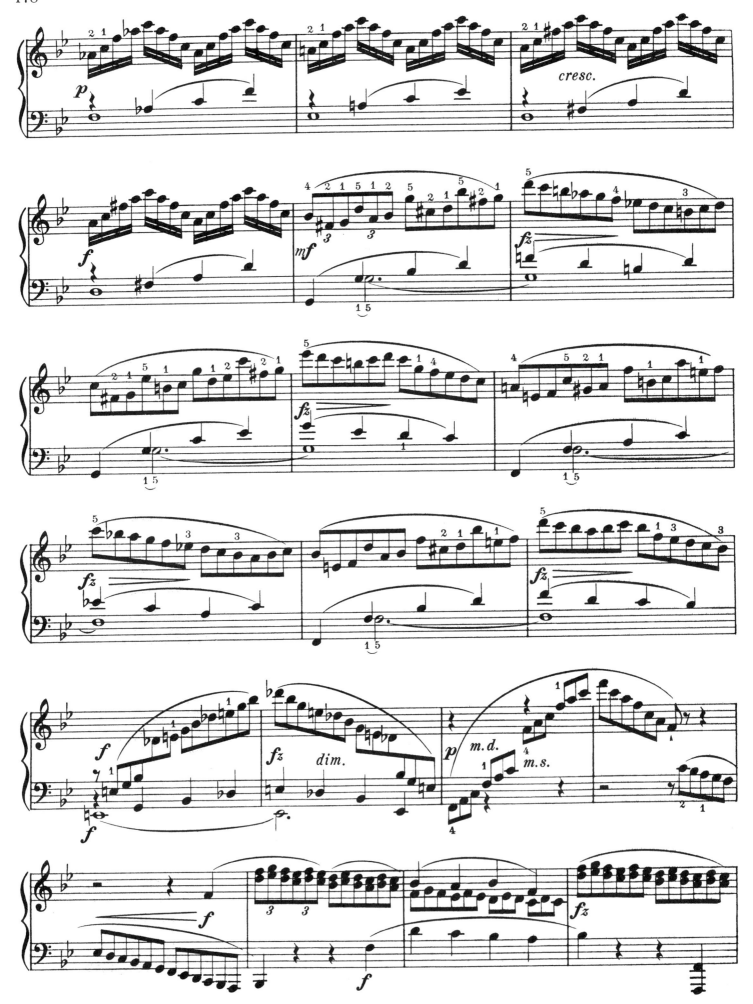